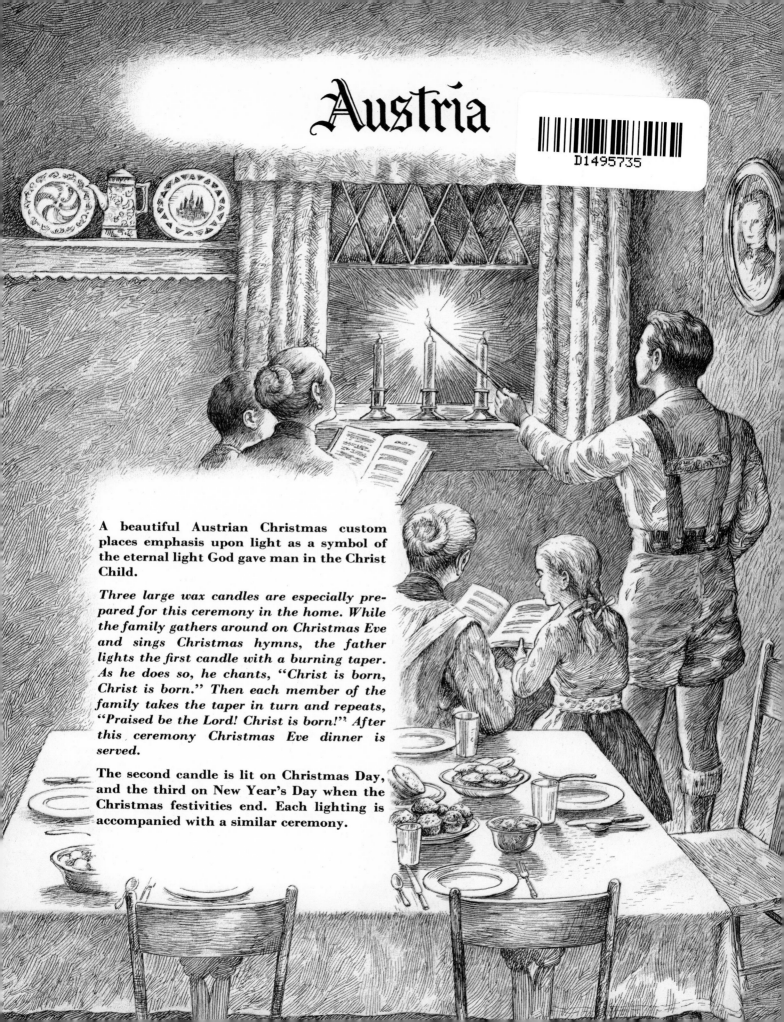

Austria

D1495735

A beautiful Austrian Christmas custom places emphasis upon light as a symbol of the eternal light God gave man in the Christ Child.

Three large wax candles are especially prepared for this ceremony in the home. While the family gathers around on Christmas Eve and sings Christmas hymns, the father lights the first candle with a burning taper. As he does so, he chants, "Christ is born, Christ is born." Then each member of the family takes the taper in turn and repeats, "Praised be the Lord! Christ is born!" After this ceremony Christmas Eve dinner is served.

The second candle is lit on Christmas Day, and the third on New Year's Day when the Christmas festivities end. Each lighting is accompanied with a similar ceremony.

Belgium

Christmas is a season of gifts and joy in Belgium. The children leave tidbits in their wooden shoes for Santa Claus' reindeer and then hang up their stockings. In the morning the oats and tidbits have disappeared — replaced with toys.

The chimes in the five-hundred-year-old cathedral in Antwerp chime ninety-nine bells on Christmas Day to summon the worshipers to services.

Hundreds of gayly-dressed, singing children precede the services in a colorful procession — carrying emblems and streamers. Priests and church dignitaries in gold-embroidered, jeweled robes follow — chanting religious songs. Ornate chariots bearing images of the Christ Child and crucifixes are featured in the procession. The procession walks on a carpet of flowers and brightly colored pieces of paper on the way to the cathedral.

Brazil

The Christmas fiesta season is solemnly heralded by an open air mass at midnight on Christmas Eve. Under brilliant tropical sky, in midsummer weather, a colorful altar is set up in the Cathedral churchyard, where the worshipers reverently pray and chant religious hymns, in a fiesta atmosphere of banners and religious trappings.

After devotions the families have Christmas Eve supper in their homes.

Bulgaria

With the appearance of the first star on Christmas Eve, the strict two weeks' fast is broken. A large round cake, called *kravai*, is decorated with the figures of a bird, a flower, and a cross, and is lighted by a candle. Incense is burned and prayers are offered before the husband and wife break a "good luck" piece from the ceremonial cake.

Christmas Day is begun with a church service, after which the children receive their gifts from Grandpa Koleda — the Bulgarian Santa Claus. As in days of old, the children present their parents with a remembrance on the eve of the last day of the old year.

Before breakfast on Christmas Day, the father of the family brings in the yule log, while the other members of the family sprinkle him with corn — a custom which is followed to bring health to all and a plenteous crop the following year. Kernels of corn are placed in a stocking, and some is also sprinkled upon the doorstep for additional assurance that the new year will be joyous. As the father lights the yule log, the children strike it, proclaiming their wishes as the sparks fly into the air.

French Canada

The charming, yet simple, declaration of Faith by the people of French Canada awakens memories of the ancient French Christmas, with its quaintness, characteristic lightness of spirit, and intense religious feeling.

Christmas day begins with a midnight mass of great splendor, followed by the Reveillon, an elaborate after-church dinner in the home. Throughout the holiday season there is great emphasis upon the religious aspects of Christmas.

On January 6th, the holiday season ends with the feast of the Kings of Epiphany, celebrated with much merriment and festivity. It is at this feast that the traditional cake, "Le Gateau des Rois" is cut. This cake has a pea and bean in it and the King and Queen of the Twelfth Night are elected by those receiving them.

China

Christmas in China is the climax of many days of Lenten preparation. Before church on Christmas Eve, the people dress in their most colorful costumes, carry their best lanterns and parade up and down the winding streets singing Christmas carols to the accompaniment of a mandolin. This singing is stopped by the burst of firecrackers announcing midnight mass, at which time the people yearly recognize the gift of the trust of children.

Chinese children call their tree the "Tree of Light" instead of a Christmas tree. Their tree has no candles but is decorated with brilliant paper flowers, colored paper chains and cotton snowflakes.

Czechoslovakia

Christmas to the people of Czechoslovakia means the ending of all quarrels and the beginning of a new year among friends. It is the custom for all people to visit their friends and foes and forgive any misunderstandings that may have arisen during the year.

Czechoslovakia of yesteryear celebrated the festive season with caroling. Carol singers were seen carrying miniature Bethlehem scenes as they sang to the people in the towns and villages and in some sections, little boys would dress in fantastic costumes, impersonating the Three Kings.

A legend still believed in is the belief that St. Nick descends from a golden cord, led by a white-clad angel. The little children go to bed early on Christmas Eve to make sure that St. Nick will stop and leave a present for them.

Denmark

"Jul-Nisse," the benevolent little man of the attic, is the essence of Christmas for many people in Denmark. Although he is seen by no one except the family cat, this little man, who lives in the attic and tends the farm animals, is responsible for many mischievous happenings in the house.

Before going to bed on Christmas Eve, the Danish children climb the attic stairs and place a bowl of porridge and a pitcher of milk before the door. They arise early the next morning, only to find that the food has mysteriously disappeared during the night.

One of Denmark's prettiest customs is the remembrance of the birds. A sheaf of grain is saved from the fall harvest — and on Christmas morning, every gable, gateway and barn door is decorated with this bundle of grain — the birds' Christmas dinner.

England

On Christmas Eve the yule log is brought inside and placed in the big fireplace. According to custom, each person in the family must sit upon the log and salute it before it is lighted to assure good luck for the household in the new year.

Religious services predominate in the English Christmas celebrations. Processions of carolers gather under the lofty arches of great cathedrals at midnight on Christmas Eve to sing the old and cherished hymns and carols. Christmas mummers are today enacting the same traditional plays which have been presented for the past several hundred years. Many of these plays, purely regional in character, bespeak Norman, Saxon, Viking and ancient British origins.

Finland

Following weeks of Christmas preparations, the Finnish house is ready for holiday celebrations by noon of Christmas Day. Suspended from the ceiling is a straw frame-work which is decorated with paper stars, suggestive of heaven. When lighted from below by the glow of the firelight and the Christmas tree candles, it produces a mysterious effect. Straw is piled upon the floor, and, reminiscent of the Christ Child, the children sleep on a manger-like bed.

In honor of the Christmas Eve celebrations, every member of the family takes a traditional "sauna," or steam bath. After the sauna, all gather about the table while the head of the family solemnly reads the Christmas prayer and sermon. The little children visit other homes during the evening, but return early to see if the man dressed as a yule goat, "Father Christmas," has left any presents for them.

Tiny candles decorate the altar and shine forth from the church windows. The merry tinkling of the bells announces the arrival of the sleighs, carrying people from near and far that they might partake of the religious services this Christmas morn.

France

Heralding the holiday season in France is St. Barbara's Day, December 6th, when watersoaked wheat grains are placed in dishes and set to germinate. An old folk legend predicts fast growing grain to mean good crops for the coming year.

The religious accent is strong upon all French Christmas customs. A miniature nativity scene, called a "Créche," is arranged by the children and placed in the living room. The créche is artistically lighted for the magnificent religious services when age-old hymns are sung, incense burned, and bells rung. Following the midnight mass, all partake of "reveillon," a luxurious meal of oysters and special wines and sausages.

A giant wicker figure, "Melchior," named after one of the Three Magi, has a basket on his back and is dressed in fantastic garb. Strapped to a donkey, he is paraded from door to door to gather whatever foods the generous may give. A candle is lighted at the church which beckons all the poor of the parish to come and receive of these gifts brought to the church by Melchior.

Germany

The immortal carol, "Silent Night, Holy Night" — Kris Kringle — hand-carved toys and the Christmas tree are only a few of the many contributions to the joyous Christmas season by the Germany of yesteryear.

The greatest contribution of all is the "Tannenbaum" — the Christmas tree — which, decorated in utmost secrecy, is lighted on Christmas Eve and is a never-failing source of enchantment and excitement for young and old alike.

Toy-giving is an important part of Christmas in Germany. Skilled hands carve toys that breathe the spirit of the bright fairyland that lies in the dark forests. Long ago, when the centers of toy-making were in the farming districts, the toys reflected objects that were familiar to the old farmsteads — houses and stables — cows and horses — woods and wild animals — carts and wagons.

Greece

December 25th is a happy day for the people of Greece, for it is the time of family reunions, parties, and merry-making. Remembering a custom of long ago, Greek mothers again make their famous fried cakes, while the little children watch in wide-eyed wonder, listening to the stories and old folk legends.

One of the most colorful legends is that of the Karkantzari — mysterious half-human and half-monster beings who wander about on the twelve days after Christmas and attempt to make mischief. The peasants call upon the priest to make the Karkantzari disappear until next year. A cross, entwined with sprigs of basil, is dipped into a copper vessel of Holy Water, and then each room of the farm house is sprinkled.

To further assure that these mysterious beings will not appear, old leather shoes, saved throughout the year, are burned, and the odor is believed to chase away these mischief-makers.

Holland

In order to provide food and water for St. Nick's good white horse on Christmas Eve, the little children of Holland stuff their clean wooden shoes with hay and carrots and place them on the window sills. A dish of water is set alongside them.

The children are up early on Christmas morning to see what St. Nick has left them, and they are always pleasantly surprised to see that St. Nick has replaced the hay and carrots with small gifts, toys and many other surprises.

After church on Christmas morning, groups of men grotesquely dressed are seen parading and singing from house to house.

In the afternoon there are family gatherings when friends visit each other and there is skating on the dikes.

Ireland

One of the most beautiful of all Christmas customs is practiced in Ireland. On Christmas Evening, candles are lighted and placed in every window of the house, and doors are left ajar. The candlelight and open door are symbols of welcomed hospitality, assuring the Irish people that no couple seeking shelter for a Baby who is the son of God will be homeless. The candlelight must shine forth all night long, and may be snuffed only by those having the name of Mary.

A cup and saucer is placed on the table in each home for the entertainment of wandering souls from purgatory, who are believed to come home for Christmas.

"Feeding the Wren" is a custom that is based upon the legend of St. Stephen who was hiding in a furze bush and betrayed to his enemies by a wren. On St. Stephen's Day, December 26th, the young children gather together, obtain a wren, and place it in a cage on top of a furze bush while they go from door to door collecting money which will be used for charity.

The United States

At Christmas time in the United States, all customs and religions stand on a common ground — the tradition of the carol. Choirs, dressed in costumes native to the countries from which they came a generation or generations ago, clearly reveal the message of the angels of, "Peace on earth and good will to all men."

Candlelight services in the churches on Christmas Eve and Christmas morning — brilliantly lighted and artistically decorated fir trees — poinsettias and mistletoe — glistening white snow — a profusion of presents — a spirit of fellowship and good will to men — the excited faces of children as they watch and wait for Santa Claus — these scenes spell Christmas in our United States.

Italy

Eclipsing the Christmas festival in Italy is the feast of the Immaculate Conception, honoring the Virgin Mary. Calabrian shepherds, dressed in goatskin trousers and colorful jackets, come down from the mountains to play on their pipes and pastoral flutes, stopping before each shrine in the streets and before the doors of all carpenter shops to salute the Virgin and Child.

Italy's Christmas scene is set with a profusion of pretty flowers and graceful olive trees. Their Santa Claus is the beneficent old witch, "Befana," who, clothed in rags, rides from house to house on a broomstick, leaving presents beside the hearth for the children.

The Precipio, truly symbolic of the Italian Christmas, is found in every home, with tiny statuettes of the Holy Family, angels, shepherds and Wise Men grouped about a miniature manger.

Mexico

A week before Christmas, street vendors display hand-carved religious figures in their booths and stalls, and tapestries of religious design are used as banners. Shepherds, following an old tradition, dress in grotesque clothes and go dancing and singing from house to house.

A pretty custom of this country is the game of the "pinata" in which the children find great joy. The "pinata" is an elaborate and colorful earthenware bowl resembling a face or an animal, filled with fresh fruits, peanuts, candy and good luck charms. When all is ready, the children gather around in a circle and one after another is blindfolded and has his turn at breaking the "pinata." After many attempts, the "pinata" is finally broken — then the scramble begins, and each child can keep whatever he manages to find.

Norway

According to tradition, church bells are heard chiming in all the cities of Norway, calling the people to five o'clock church on Christmas Eve — December 24th — when the Christmas celebrations begin.

Many weeks before, the families are busy making gifts for Christmas and preparing food to be stored against the long winter. Cheese and sausages are made; breads and animal-shaped cookies are baked; little colored candles for the tree are finished; and the "lutefisk" is ready.

One of the most charming customs of Norway is the remembrance of the animals and birds, since they were the only ones present at the birth of the Holy Babe. The farm beasts are carefully tended, and the cattle are given extra fodder. But the most beautiful of all the customs is saved for the birds. The especially gleaned sheaf, saved from the fall harvest, is placed on top of a tall pole in the yard — and on Christmas morning, every gable, gateway and barn door is decorated with a bundle of grain — the birds' Christmas dinner.

Palestine

Members of all denominations assemble to worship and sing carols in the Church of the Nativity in Bethlehem—directly above the birthplace of the Holy Child.

As of old, the Church is ablaze with flags and decorations on Christmas Evening, and men and women crowd doors and windows, even standing upon the square, flat house tops to view the spectacle. A signal from the watcher at the highest point announces the coming of the procession which is dramatically heralded by a flying horseman holding aloft a streaming banner. A corps of native police, mounted upon fiery Arabian horses is followed by a solitary horseman standing upon a coal-black steed, carrying the cross on high. Following and completing the procession are the cortege of church men and native government, and the two-wheeled carriages with their picturesque Oriental Jehus.

The procession solemnly enters the church. Because the placing of the ancient effigy of the Holy Child cannot be seen by the public, the people move forward in the church, pass behind the high altars, and down the steep, winding steps which lead to the grotto. Here, marked by a silver star, is the site of the birth of Jesus. Here, too, is the site of the manger where the Holy Babe lay.

Philippine Islands

Colorful wreaths and chains, made of brilliant tropical flowers, are worn by the Filipino children as they partake in the festive after-mass parade. A band leads the parade, providing the music for the children's singing.

In keeping with the significant religious spirit of the Christmas season, a family dinner follows the after-mass parade. Dancing and musical entertainment provide the remaining celebrations for the afternoon and evening.

The Filipino children do not have a Christmas tree — but they decorate their homes with lavish care. Flags, bunting, palms, and the many colorful flowers adorn their homes, and a candle is kept burning in the window all night long.

Concluding the celebrations of Christmas day, melodious church bells are heard ringing throughout the land until the last stroke of the clock proclaims that Christmas day has ended.

Poland

One of the most beautiful celebrations of the religious traditions of Christmas is offered to the world by Poland.

When the first star appears in the evening sky on December 24, Fast Day is ended and the Christmas supper begins. Straw is placed under the table, dishes, and tablecloth, and one chair is left vacant for the Holy Child. Symbolizing peace on earth is the Peace Wafer, procured from the priest and given to the head of the family to break and share with the guests. While the sacred wafer is being eaten, wishes for the coming year are exchanged.

Puppet shows, called "schopka," depicting the murder of the Innocents by Herod, are given during the holidays. It is said that on Christmas night the heavens open and those who have lived pure and blameless lives can see the vision of Jacob's ladder.

The Polish Christmas centers around the songs which are a combination of the religious and secular sentiments of the people, sung in memory of the Savior's birth.

Rumania

Throughout the Christmas season many dramatic remembrances of the story of Christ's birth are enacted. From dawn until after sunset on the day before Christmas, boys visit neighboring homes to sing a Christmas greeting, "Colinde," for which they receive apples, cakes, and coins. On Christmas Day they parade through the streets carrying a great wooden cross which is hung with little tinkling bells. The star is illuminated from within by a candle, and is decorated with a transparency of the Baby Jesus and the Magi Kings.

Roast pig is the principal food of the Christmas dinner, and is served with "colaci," a wheat loaf, and a symbolic cake called "turta." Layers of thin dough are shaped to form leaves, which are representative of the Christ Child's swaddling clothes.

An ancient, but still practiced Rumanian custom is "Blessing the Danube." Clad in gay costumes to depict Pontius Pilate, Herod, and other biblical characters, the people gather at the river bank to sing carols. A young boy breaks the ice and a wooden cross is thrown into the water. All scramble after it, for the rescuer will have extraordinary fortune in the coming year.

Russia

Many of Russia's traditions have been lost and forgotten, but family reunions and parties for the children during the Christmas season still remain. At these reunions, an old custom — the Five Piles of Grain — is enacted. At midnight, a sleeping hen is taken from the roost and brought into the warm kitchen. On the floor are five piles of grain, each one representing a legend of the five fates: Wealth, Poverty, Death, Marriage and a life of Single Blessedness. While the hen is still sleepy, its befuddlement causes great merriment and laughter, but as the hen awakens and senses the grain, she selects the piles, one by one and begins to eat.

The many celebrations which are associated with Christmas in Russia are especially interesting and valuable because they reflect customs of the past. Processions of carolers are heard singing the old "kolyada" songs which refer to pagan deities and a "badnyak," a piece of wood similar to the yule log, is solemnly burnt on Christmas Eve to keep away evil spirits.

Serbia

On Christmas Day friends call upon neighbors to "let Christmas in." Upon entering the house, the caller sprinkles handfuls of grain in the corners of the house to assure bountiful crops the coming year.

He then strikes the burning yule log with a poker and as the sparks fly, makes a wish for good fortune to the family. The caller then kneels down and kisses one end of the log, as he places a coin on it as his Christmas gift to his good neighbor.

Sicily

Mountain musicians, playing melancholy melodies upon a violin and cello as they stroll through the village streets, set the picturesque Christmas scene in Sicily.

A pyramid-shaped altar, adorned with a waxen image of the Christ Child, is built in each home and church. Every evening, for nine days before Christmas, the altar is lighted and the people proclaim their devotion. Carols are sung in the homes, while in the church, strolling musicians perform scenes from the story of Christ's birth in the lowly manger.

A midnight mass is held on Christmas Eve. Following the religious service and carol singing, the people form a procession which is led by the priest, carrying the waxen image of the Christ Child. As the procession slowly winds through the town, fires are lighted in the squares — church bells are rung — and rockets are sent up to the sky.

After the "birth of the bambino" has been acclaimed by all, good wishes are exchanged and all return to their homes to enjoy the delicacies of the Christmas dinner.

Spain

Plump turkeys, quacking ducks, and cooing pigeons crowd the Christmas markets which are a special feature of Spain's festive season. Streets and plazas are lined with stalls heaped high with oranges, melons, colored flowers, children's toys, and "turron, mazapon" and other candies. Amidst floods of music and laughter, dark-eyed eager children run from booth to booth to gaze in wonder at the array.

Preceding the midnight "Nocha Buena" mass, the little children dress in peasant costumes and enact an age-long Christmas Eve tradition of dancing around the Nativity scene to the musical accompaniment of tambourines.

According to an old Spanish tradition, the Magi are said to journey to Bethlehem every year. And so, on Epiphany Eve, the children are laden with gifts as they wait at the city gates to meet the Kings. They look for the group in the sunset, but soon the glorious vision fades away and the children turn homeward, believing the Kings to have passed behind the mountains.

Spanish children have no Christmas tree and do not hang up their stockings on Christmas Eve. Instead, they practice a custom called "nacimiento" which means hiding slippers and shoes for Balthasar and the Wise Men to fill with goodies.

Sweden

St. Lucia, dressed in white with a brilliant red sash about her waist, and wearing an astonishing crown of pine boughs haloed with the light of seven candles, awakens the members of the household by bringing them coffee and cakes on a tray, thereby proclaiming the arrival of the Christmas season on December 13th.

A belief of Sweden is that ancestors come back to their former homes on Christmas Eve; and so, according to tradition, the living behave as intruders for the night as they make up the beds and prepare the tables for their ancestors.

Swedish holiday celebrations end on Christmas Eve with tree-trimming, dancing, singing, a dinner of "lutefisk," and the opening of the Christmas presents which are sealed with red wax.

Switzerland

"Samichlaus," as he is known in Switzerland, is eagerly awaited by the children on December 5th. In the mountain hamlets he is heralded with a procession from the little village church. Cross-bearer and banner boys, wearing quaint, high-peaked hoods for protection from the mountain air and snow, lead the choir and clergy through the street. In their midst is the Saint himself — Samichlaus — wearing a red, jovial mask, white flowing beard, fur-trimmed robe, and a gray sack and staff, both conveying rewards for the good and bad children.

Samichlaus is met in the streets of the larger cities by happy, applauding children. He is usually a young bishop, accompanied by grotesquely masked attendant bishops carrying the triple purse associated with St. Nicholas. While the good bishop distributes apples and cookies, the attendant bishops collect alms.

Syria

Christmas Eve in Syria is spent in worship and prayer. On this evening a bonfire of vine stems is made in the middle of each church, in memory of the Magi who were cold from their journey.

Many Syrians journey to nearby Bethlehem to attend the midnight service in the Holy Land. Christmas Day is chiefly observed in the home with prayers and quiet rejoicing. Young boys and girls, masked and dressed in gay costume, go singing from door to door and receive coins, eggs, and candies in return.

Much laughter and merrymaking accompany New Year's Day. Legend tells that a camel, the youngest of those bearing the Wise Men, fell down, exhausted by the journey. The Christ Child blessed it and conferred immortality upon it. For this reason, the Syrian Santa Claus is the camel, who brings gifts to the children on New Year's Day. Before going to bed that night, little boys and girls set a bowl of water and wheat outside the house; in the morning, the good find gifts, and the naughty find a black mark on their wrists.

Yugoslavia

Men of the family rise before dawn on the day before Christmas to search in the forests for a young oak tree, suitable for their "Badnyak," or yule log. Many traditions must be adhered to regarding the log. It must fall toward the east at the moment of sunrise—if any branches touch another tree it is an omen of bad luck for the coming year. Upon their arrival home, the men are greeted with song and feted with a light supper. To allow the log to die out would mean misfortune in the coming year, so certain members of the family keep an all night vigil.

A fire is built and the family gathers around the burning log to await the arrival of "polaznik," a village lad, who must be the first to enter the house on Christmas morning. Entering, polaznik throws a handful of grain at each member of the family, asking a blessing as he does so. Next, the log is struck so that many sparks fly into the air, each spark meaning many sheep, cattle, and pigs.

Concluding this ritual, polaznik pours some wine on the log, leaving a coin on one end to assure the family of bounteous living in the new year. In return for his blessings, polaznik is treated with food and is entertained in the home for the remainder of the Christmas day.